GUITAR SPRINGBOARD by Michael Morenga

Beats For Beginners

The basics of rhythm guitar

Boston Music Company
part of The Music Sales Group
New York/Los Angeles/Nashville/London/Berlin/Copenhagen/Madrid/Paris/Sydney/Tokyo

Published by
Boston Music Company

Exclusive Distributors:
Music Sales Corporation
257 Park Avenue South, New York, NY 10010 USA

Music Sales Limited
14-15 Berners Street, London W1T 3LJ England

Music Sales Pty. Limited
120 Rothschild Street, Rosebery, Sydney, NSW 2018, Australia

Order No. BMC-12067
ISBN 0-8256-8222-3

This book © Copyright 2006 Boston Music Company,
A division of Music Sales Corporation, New York

Translated & edited by Rebecca Taylor.

Printed in the United States of America

Your Guarantee of Quality:
As publishers, we strive to produce every book
to the highest commercial standards.

The book has been carefully designed to minimize awkward page turns
and to make playing from it a real pleasure. Particular care has been given
to specifying acid-free, neutral-sized paper made from pulps
which have not been elemental chlorine bleached.

This pulp is from farmed sustainable forests and
was produced with special regard for the environment.

Throughout, the printing and binding have been planned
to ensure a sturdy, attractive publication which should give
years of enjoyment.

If your copy fails to meet our high standards, please inform us
and we will gladly replace it.

www.musicsales.com

SM   Contents

Introduction

Let's set the scene: you've picked up your guitar, figured out how to hold it, and now you want to start playing your favorite tunes. The only trouble is you can't read the rhythms properly, which is fine if you already know how the whole song goes, but tricky if you don't, and makes it almost impossible to learn new pieces! A good sense of rhythm is one of the most important yet most fundamental elements of a guitarist's technique, and this book will help you master it quickly and easily.

Over the following pages, you will be introduced to all the different note values up to and including the sixteenth note, as well as some techniques you can use to help you to play rhythms more accurately, information on the most common time signatures, and playing legato and staccato passages. There is a handy diagram at the back of the book if at any stage you find you need to remind yourself of the basics. Let's start by discovering exactly what rhythm is.

The three elements of music

Music is made up of three different elements:

- Melody (a sequence of notes at different intervals or at the same pitch)
- Harmony (chords, chord sequences)
- Rhythm (the variation of the duration of melody or harmony over time)

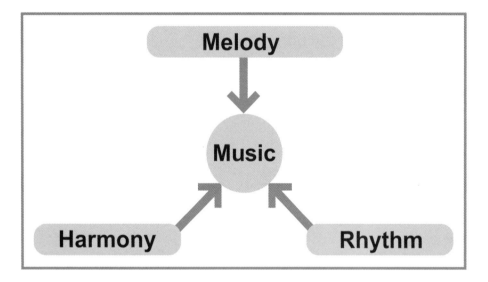

What is rhythm?

Rhythm is:

- A sequence of events within organized time
- Notes and sounds ordered in a particular manner, defined either by note values, time signatures, or tempo

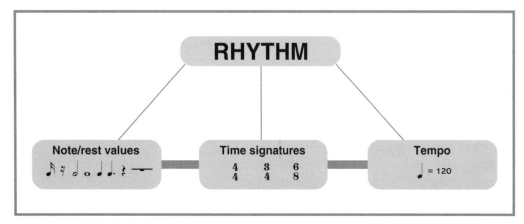

Most music is written using time signatures. A time signature specifies how many beats are in each bar and which note value constitutes one beat. It appears at the beginning of a piece of music just after the clef.

The most common time signature is ⁴₄. Each bar is separated into four beats, which are counted as "1–2–3–4," and constitute a quarter note each. The first and third beats are known as strong beats (or "onbeats") and the second and fourth beats are known as weak beats (or "offbeats").

One way of keeping a strong rhythmic feel and a regular tempo (speed) is to use your foot as a metronome:

● Tap your foot on each of the four beats, on each quarter note of the ⁴₄ bar

● Lift your foot on the count of "and"

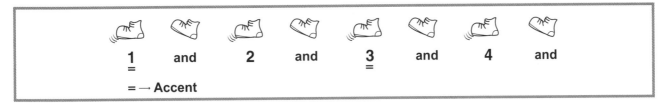

Practice the following exercise without an instrument:

● Set the tempo (not too fast to start with!) by counting two bars out loud: "1, 2, 3, 4 – 1, 2, 3, 4." After the second "4" (or better still, on the "4 and"), lift your foot.

● On the next "1" tap your foot and clap your hands. It is important to make sure your spoken introduction is in the same tempo as the following bars!

● Then, in the same tempo, lift your foot on the count of "and" and tap it down again on the count of "2," clapping your hands at the same time.

● Complete the whole bar in this way, remembering to accent the strong beats ("1" and "3"). Keep going as long as you can, and practice this a few times every day.

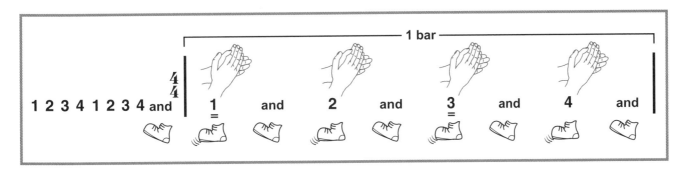

● You can practice this exercise standing up or sitting down. The spoken introduction is important to help you establish a regular tempo. Make sure you always count two bars out loud first.

● Using a metronome will help you to practice the rhythms in a controlled manner. Your goal should be to synchronize your foot-tapping and hand-clapping with the metronome clicks. A slow tempo is recommended to start with!

● A very good way to practice rhythms is to count the beats out loud at the same time. This will help you to concentrate on the rhythm and see where the beats lie.

● First, try practicing without an instrument to get used to the rhythms.

Strumming hand stopping techniques

There are a variety of techniques which can help you play rhythms fast and accurately. If you learn these techniques properly, you will find they can help you play in many different musical styles.

Palm stopping

The first technique is used to play a rest after having played a note and is a stopping technique known as "palm stopping." This technique is also useful for playing staccato (staccato = separated, played short).

- By lightly resting on all the strings, the ball of the hand stops the sound after playing a note
- This technique is especially useful for switching between notes and rests

Palm muting

Another useful stopping technique is called "palm muting." This technique is widespread in rock and metal music and is particularly suited to playing eighth notes (☞ pages 16–17).

The alternation of muting and releasing the strings can help with playing accents (☞ page 18) and also helps define staccato passages.

- Rest the heel of your picking hand lightly on the strings close to the bridge and use your pick to play the chord
- Then, gently raise the ball of your hand at the same time as strumming
- The notes should sound normally again

Fretting hand stopping techniques

Notes can also be stopped using the fretting hand. This is less clumsy and therefore much more suitable for playing stopped notes very quickly.

Ghost notes

A "ghost note" is played by fretting a note and not picking it. This technique can add interesting new tone colors to the music. It is also used to achieve a percussive effect when the strumming hand is playing a rhythm.

- A chord (in this case E7) can be silenced by decreasing the pressure of the fingers on the fretboard

- Use the fingers which are not playing the chord to dampen the remaining strings

- In order to achieve a clean, percussive ghost note, one finger can be left as a support on a string while the pressure of the remaining fingers is decreased

- This will make the notes sound quieter

- Palm muting is good to practice using two-note power chords (☞ *GUITAR SPRINGBOARD: Chords For All Occasions*) and rock eighth notes (☞ page 17).

- Ghost notes can be practiced without gripping the neck of the guitar. You can get the feel for the technique by practicing placing the four fingers of the fretting hand gently over the strings.

Tips

7

Whole notes

A whole note is a note held for four beats: in $\frac{4}{4}$ time, this is a whole bar. Practice playing the figure below and counting the beats out loud as you do so.

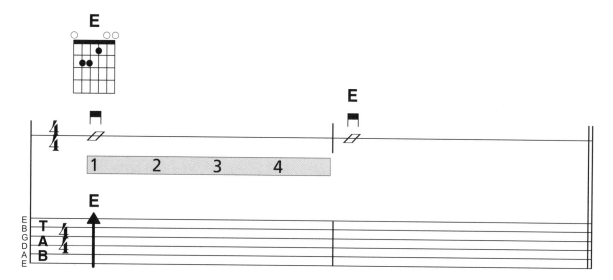

Exercise 1

Try playing through the passage below, taking care to make the chord changes accurate.

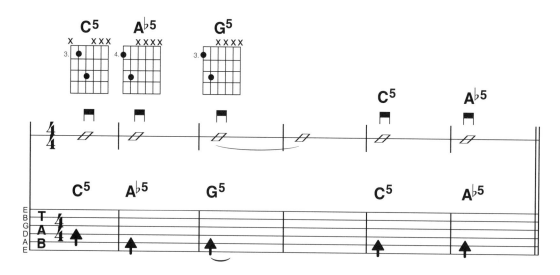

Tip: the arrow length shows you how many strings to strum

Tips

- When strumming the chords, make sure you play them exactly on the first beat of each bar.

- Each chord should sound until the end of the bar. At first, you may find it helpful to count "4 and 1" to get the hang of this.

- In the example above, the tie joins one whole note to another. This means that the chord should be held for two bars and not re-struck.

- Tricky chord changes should be practiced beforehand in a "loop" without a metronome (e.g. alternate two chords continuously).

- When practicing with a metronome, start the tempo at around ♩=100.

A whole-note rest is a silence lasting four beats: in $\frac{4}{4}$ time, this is a whole bar. Practice playing the figure below and counting the beats out loud as you do so.

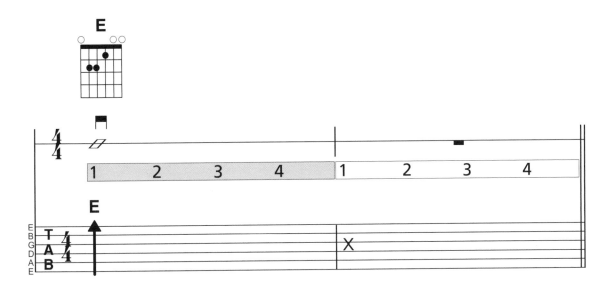

Try playing through the passage below, taking care to make the chord changes accurate. Watch out for the rest in bar 4!

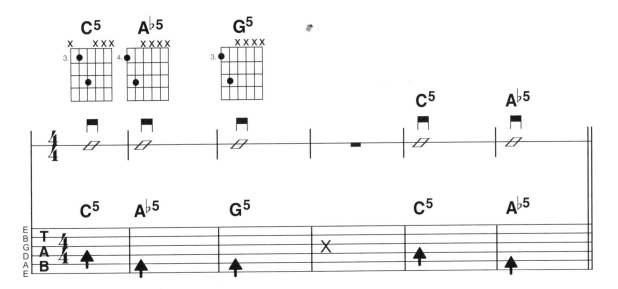

- Make sure you always play the chords exactly on the first beat of each bar.

- Ensure each chord sounds until the end of the bar. At first, you may find it helpful to count "4 and 1" to get the hang of this.

- The rest in bar 4 of the example above means that this bar should be silent. The strings are stopped on count "1" with the strumming hand (☞ Strumming hand stopping technique, page 6).

- Tricky chord changes should be practiced beforehand in a loop without a metronome (e.g. alternate two chords continuously).

- When practicing with a metronome, start the tempo at around ♩=100.

Tips

Half notes

A half note is a note played for two beats: in ⁴⁄₄ time, this is half a bar. Practice playing the figure below and counting the beats out loud as you do so.

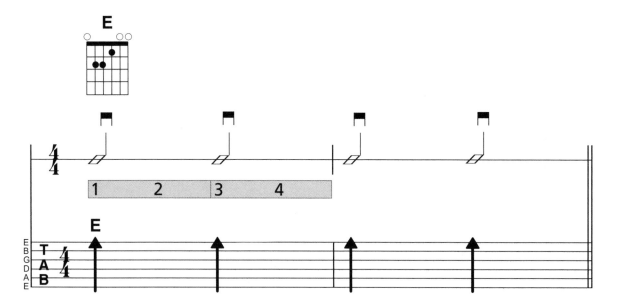

Exercise 3: sequence of half notes using chords in the first position

Try playing through the passage below, taking care to make the chord changes accurate. Watch out for the two chord changes in the last bar.

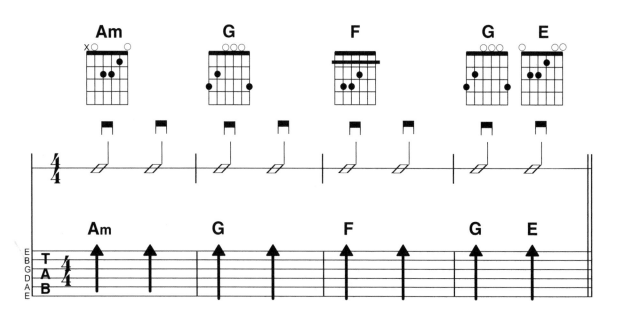

Tips

- Counting the beats out loud will help you to maintain a sense of rhythm. Say "1" and "3" slightly louder, because these are so-called strong beats which should be accented slightly when playing.

- Make sure each chord sounds until the end of the bar. At first, you may find it useful to count "4 and 1" to get the hang of this.

- Tricky chord changes should be practiced beforehand in a loop without a metronome (e.g. alternate two chords continuously).

- When practicing with a metronome, start the tempo at around ♩=100.

A half-note rest is a silence of two beats: in ⁴⁄₄ time, this is half a bar. Practice playing the figure below and counting the beats out loud as you do so.

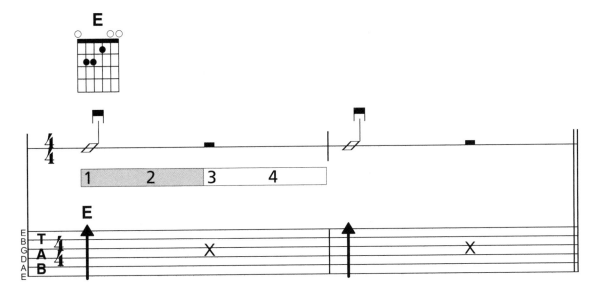

Try playing through the passage below, taking care to make the chord changes accurate. Watch out for the two chord changes in the last bar and use the rests to prepare for the chord changes in bars 1 to 3.

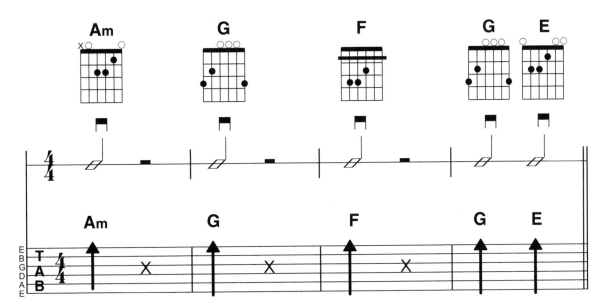

- Stop the sound of all six strings on the count of "3" using the strumming hand stopping technique (☞ page 6).
- Wherever you see a rest sign, no chord should be audible.
- Tricky chord changes should be practiced beforehand in a loop without a metronome (e.g. alternate two chords continuously).
- When practicing with a metronome, start the tempo at around ♩=100.

Tips

Legato quarter notes

A quarter note is a note played for one beat: in ¼ time, this is a quarter of a bar. Practice playing the figure below and count the beats out loud as you do so.

You will notice that there are short lines underneath all the noteheads below. These indicate the notes should be held for their full value and is called "legato." When playing legato, the sound of the first note should continue right up until the following note. The symbol for this in guitar music is usually a line underneath or above the notehead.

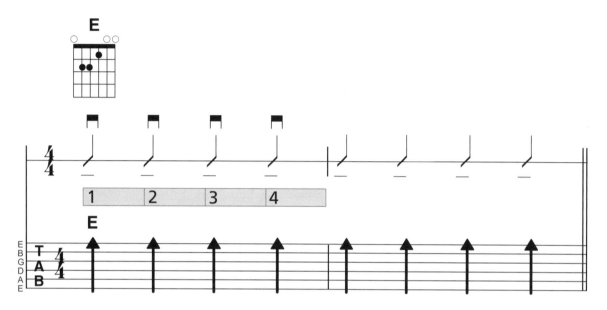

Legato quarter notes with chord changes

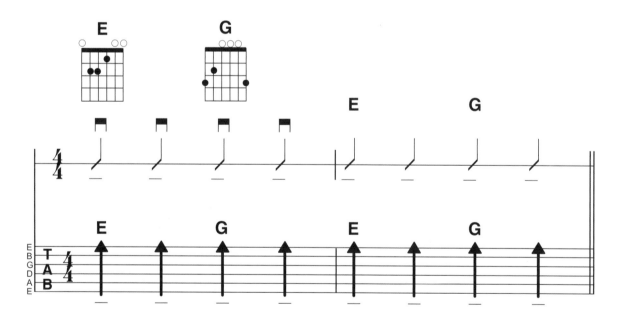

Tips

- It is sometimes hard to make legato playing sound rhythmical and therefore it is best to practice with a metronome, making sure that the chord changes are well defined.

- When practicing with a metronome, start the tempo at around ♩=76.

Rather than lines, you will notice that the quarter notes in the following passage have dots underneath. This indicates the note should be played short and is called "staccato" (staccato = short, separated). The sound of the chord or note does not continue right up until the following note like legato playing. Instead, it is stopped shortly after playing (☞ Strumming hand stopping technique, page 6). The symbol for this in guitar music is a dot underneath or above the notehead.

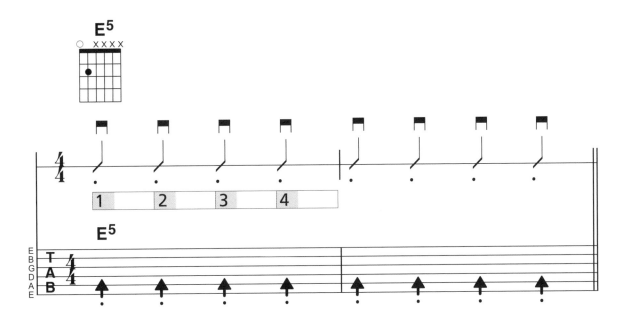

Staccato quarter notes with chord changes

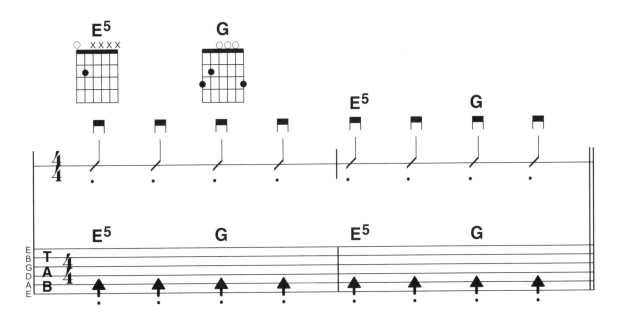

- Stop the sound of the strings on all six strings shortly after the note is struck, using the strumming hand stopping technique (☞ page 6).

- The staccato technique makes rhythms sound marked and dynamic.

- When practicing with a metronome, start the tempo at around ♩=76.

Tips

13

Muted strums

There are other ways of adding interest to music rather than simple variation of note values and pitches. One method is to add some textural variation. To do this you can use muted strums (☞ page 7). In the example below, beats "2" and "4" are played in this manner. This creates a snare drum-like off-beat effect.

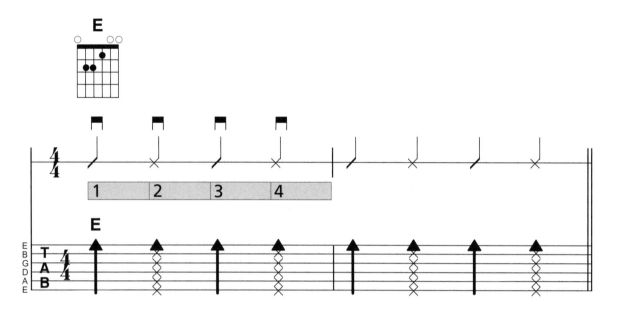

Muted strums with chord changes

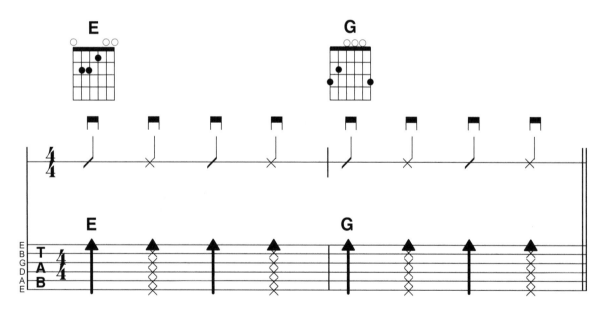

Tips

- The quarter notes sounding on beats "1" and "3" should be played for their whole duration, while the percussive notes (beats "2" and "4") should sound shorter and more detached.

- When practicing with a metronome, start the tempo at around ♩=76.

A quarter-note rest is a silence of one beat: in $\frac{4}{4}$ time, this is a quarter of a bar. Practice playing the figure below and count the beats out loud as you do so.

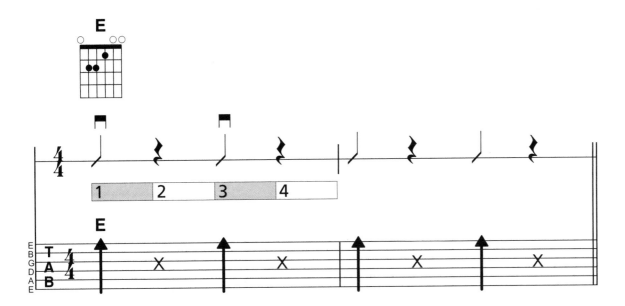

Quarter notes and quarter-note rests with chord changes

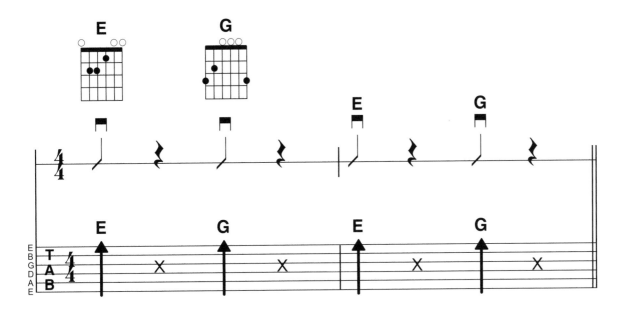

- Stop the sound of all six strings on beats "2" and "4" using the strumming hand stopping technique (☞ page 6).

- Tricky chord changes should be practiced beforehand in a loop without a metronome (e.g. alternate two chords continuously).

- When practicing with a metronome, start the tempo at around ♩=76.

Tips

Eighth notes

An eighth note is a note played for half a beat. Practice playing the figure below and count the beats out loud as you do so.

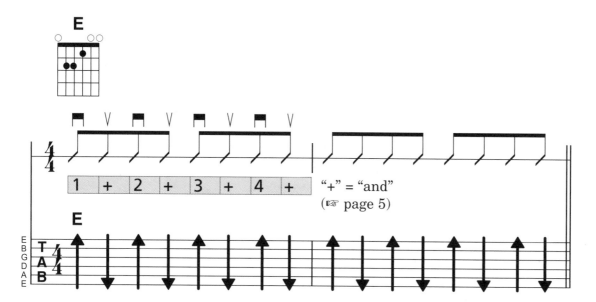

"+" = "and"
(☞ page 5)

Eighth notes with chord changes

Now that you have mastered simple eighth notes, let's try incorporating some chord changes. Make sure the changes below are accurate and always appear exactly on the first and third beats.

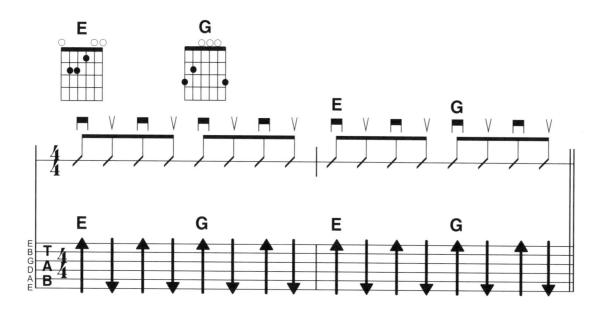

Tips

- A low action and good timing of the fingers is essential for playing even eighth notes.

- Treat these exercises as endurance tests. Continuous eighth notes can, for example, be practiced for a "target time" of three minutes using a metronome.

- Tricky chord changes should be practiced beforehand in a loop without a metronome (e.g. alternate two chords continuously).

- When practicing with a metronome, start the tempo at around ♩=76.

If you have ever been to a rock concert, you may have noticed that the guitarists often play eighth notes just using downstrokes. Practice the example below, slowly at first, until you can play the eighth notes evenly.

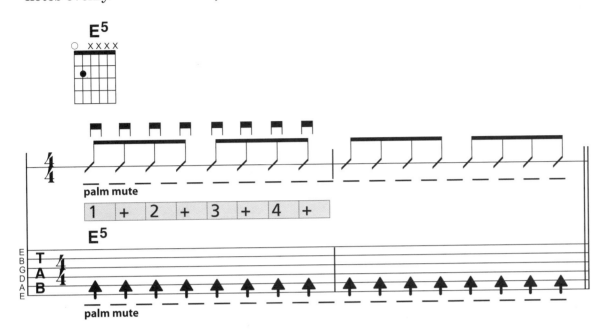

Rock eighth notes with chord changes

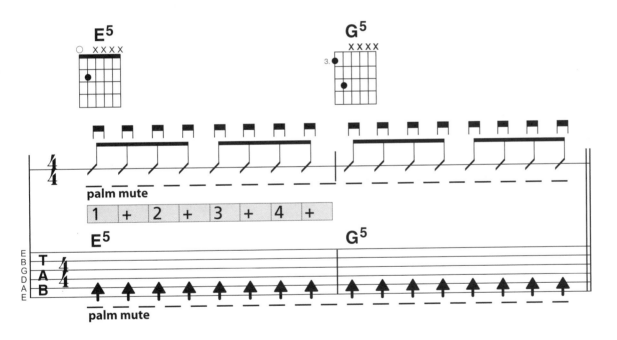

- A low action and good timing of the fingers is essential for playing even eighth notes. Treat these exercises as endurance tests. Continuous eighth notes can, for example, be practiced for a target time of three minutes using a metronome.

- Tricky chord changes should be practiced beforehand in a loop without a metronome (e.g. alternate two chords continuously).

- When practicing with a metronome, start the tempo at around ♩=76.

Tips

Accents

An accent is the emphasis of a note or chord and can help produce a variety of rhythmic effects. Accents are written for guitar using the symbol >. Practice the example below, accenting the first, fourth, and seventh eighth notes of each bar. You might have to start at a very slow speed until you get the hang of it!

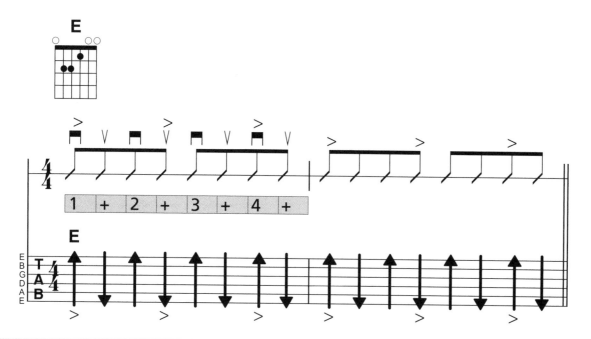

Eighth notes with accents and chord changes

Now try the same thing with chord changes.

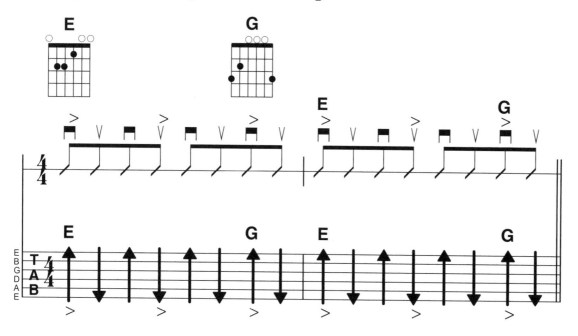

Tips

- Accents generate a second rhythmic pulse in addition to the basic rhythm.
- When practicing, you could try isolating the accents from the notes themselves and rehearsing them, for example, as a hand-clapping exercise, using your foot as a metronome.
- When practicing with a metronome, start the tempo at around ♩ = 76.

An eighth-note rest is a silence lasting half a beat. Practice playing the figure below and count the beats out loud as you do so.

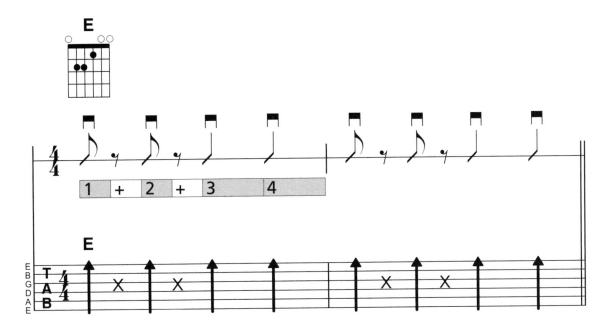

Eighth notes and eighth-note rests with chord changes

Now try the same thing with chord changes.

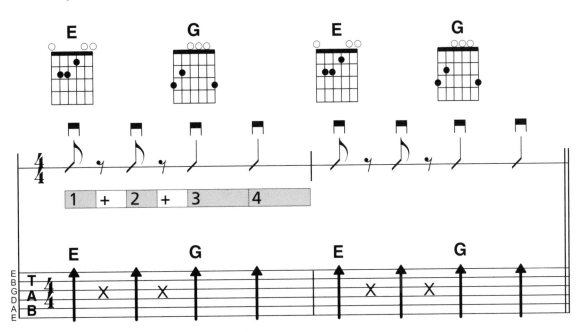

- Stop the sound of all six strings on beats "2" and "4" using the strumming hand stopping technique (☞ page 6).

- Tricky chord changes should be practiced beforehand in a loop without a metronome (e.g. alternate two chords continuously).

- When practicing with a metronome, start the tempo at around ♩=76.

Tips

Syncopation

Syncopation is the shifting of an accent from a strong beat (for example beat "1" in bar 2 of the passage below) to a weak beat (for example beat "4 and" of the example below) or vice versa.

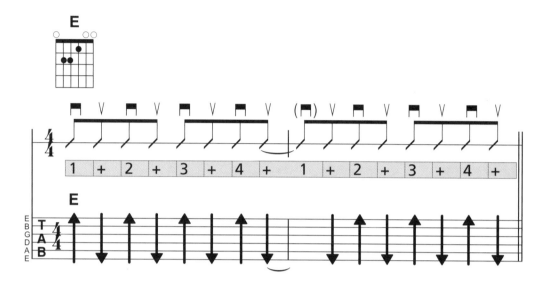

Syncopation with chord changes

Now try the same thing with chord changes.

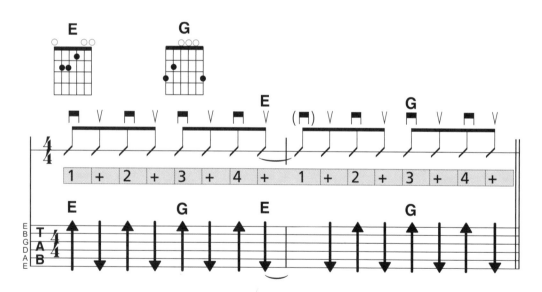

Tips

- Syncopations always occur on unaccented beats.
- When playing tied eighth notes, you might find the air strumming technique useful (notated above using brackets). Instead of actually striking the strings, imitate the stroke just above the strings. This should help you to stay in tempo.
- When practicing with a metronome, start the tempo at around ♩=76.

When a dot is placed next to a note, the note increases its value by half. For example:

- Half note or half-note rest with dot: 2 + 1 = 3 beats (☞ page 31)
- Quarter note or quarter-note rest with dot: $1 + \frac{1}{2} = 1\frac{1}{2}$ beats (☞ page 31)

Practice the example below, being careful to play the notes for their exact value.

Dotted half notes and dotted half-note rests

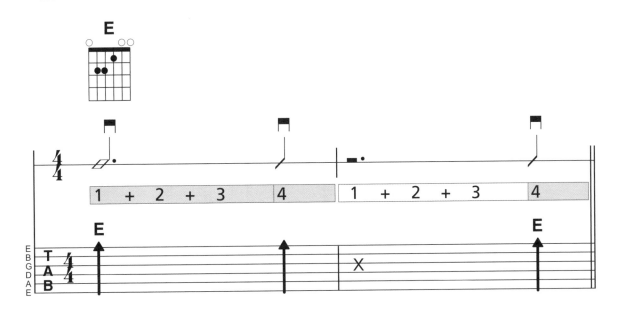

Dotted quarter notes and dotted quarter-note rests

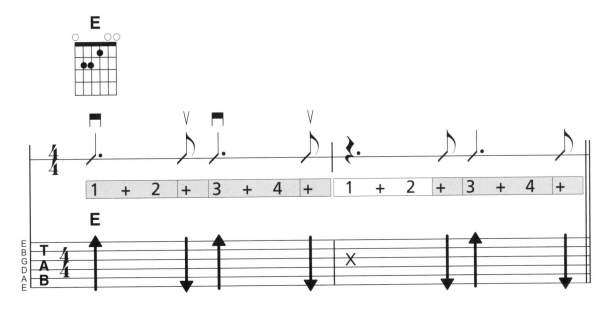

- Clap the rhythm to start with, in order to get a feel for the eighth note on beat "2 +."
- Tricky passages should be isolated and practiced beforehand in a loop without a metronome (e.g. repeat the passage continuously).
- When practicing with a metronome, start the tempo at around ♩=76.

Tips

21

Exercises combining different note values

We have now covered all the note values up to and including eighth notes. Play the following exercise slowly at first, counting out loud as you go. Don't let the chord change in the second bar take you by surprise!

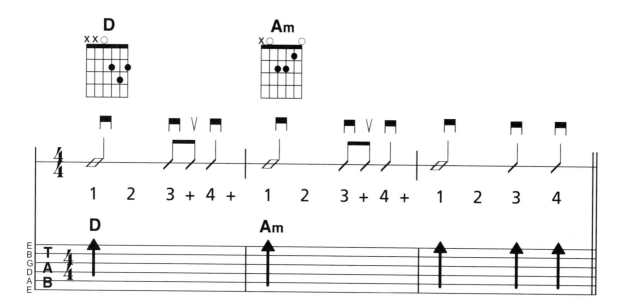

Combining different note values with chord changes

Now let's try incorporating some rests. Count out loud, and try to use the rests to prepare for the chord changes.

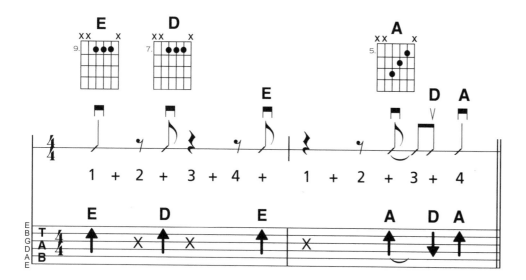

Tips

- You will notice that the passages above include a variety of different note values. In order to get the hang of the tricky rhythms you may find it helpful to count out the beats beforehand.

- Alternatively, you could practice without an instrument by clapping your hands and using your foot as a metronome.

- When practicing with a metronome, start the tempo at around ♩=76.

Triplets are groups of three notes of equal value. They are often found in swing and boogie-woogie.

A group of three triplet eighth notes is equal to a group of two normal eighth notes. Practice the exercise below, counting "one and a two and a three and a four and a" to help you play notes of equal value.

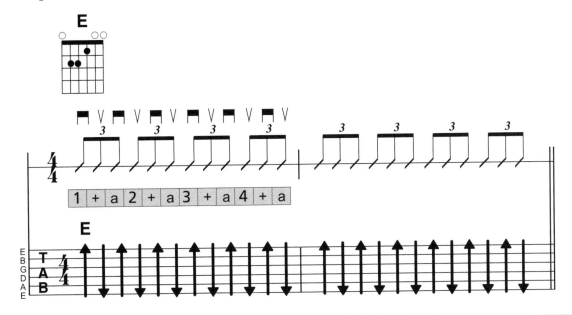

Quarter-note triplets work on the same principle as eighth-note triplets, except a group of three triplet quarter-notes is equal to a group of two normal quarter notes. The exercise below should sound like a slowed-down version of the triplet eighth note pattern above.

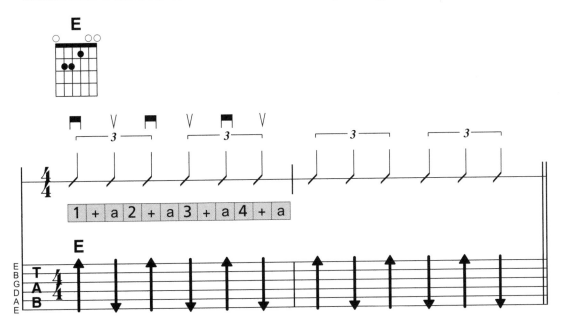

- The final chord should sound right until the end of the bar. To start with, count "4 and 1" to make sure you are holding it for its full length.

- Tricky chord changes should be practiced beforehand in a loop without a metronome (e.g. alternate two chords continuously).

- When practicing with a metronome, start the tempo at around ♩=76.

Tips

23

Sixteenth notes

A sixteenth note is equal to half an eighth note and occupies a sixteenth of a ⁴⁄₄ bar. Practice the exercises on the next two pages, paying particular attention to the changing note values and the strumming marks.

Continuous sixteenth notes

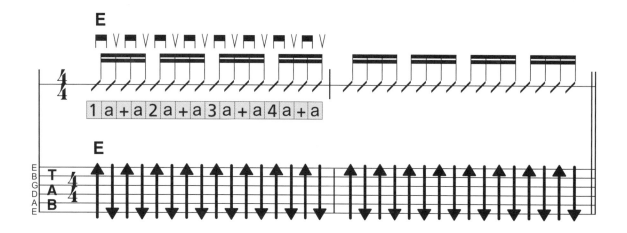

Eighth–sixteenth–sixteenth

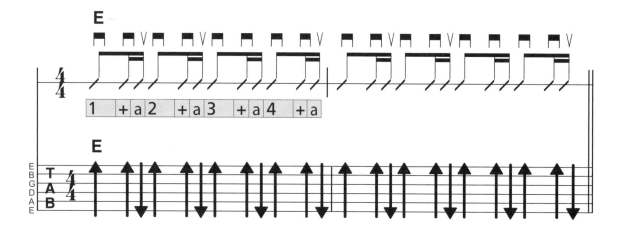

Sixteenth–sixteenth–eighth

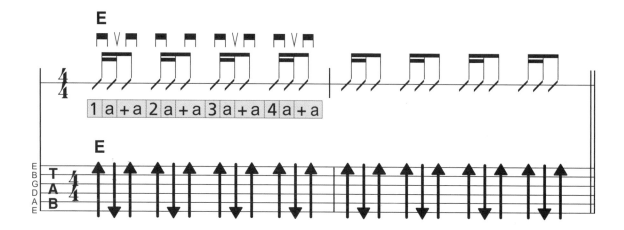

24

Sixteenth notes

Sixteenth–eighth–sixteenth

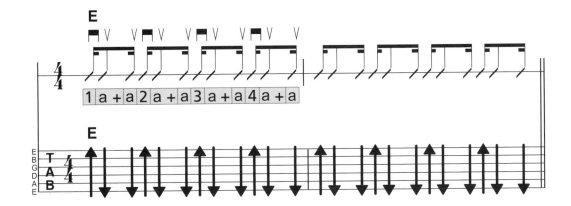

Dotted eighth–sixteenth

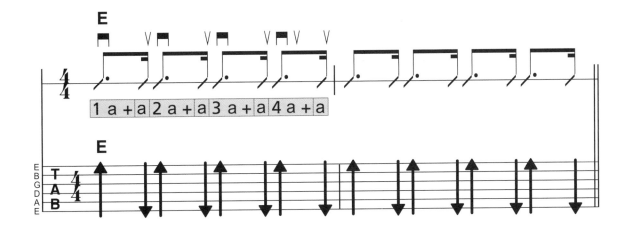

Sixteenth–dotted eighth

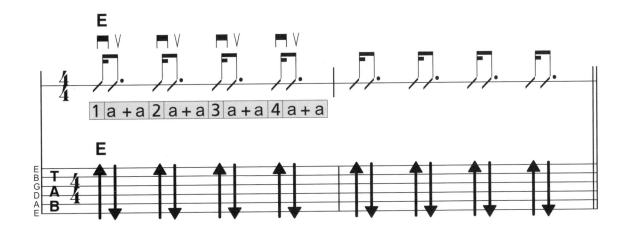

Sixteenth-note rests

A sixteenth-note rest is a silence of half an eighth-note rest and occupies a sixteenth of a $\frac{4}{4}$ bar. Practice the exercises on the next two pages, paying particular attention to the changing note values and the strumming marks.

Sixteenth-note rests 1

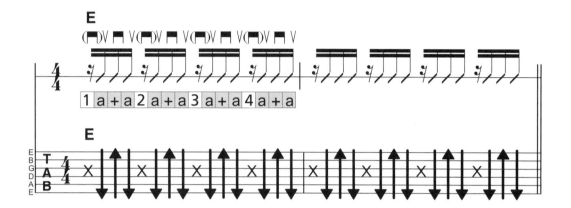

Sixteenth-note rests 2

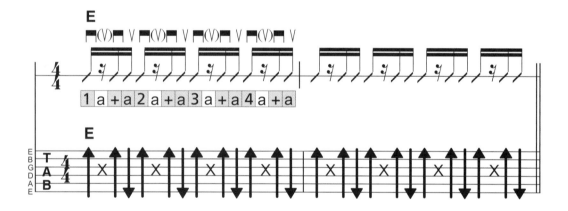

Sixteenth-note rests 3

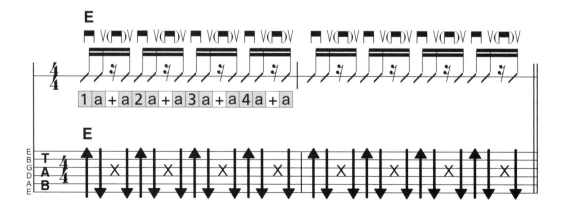

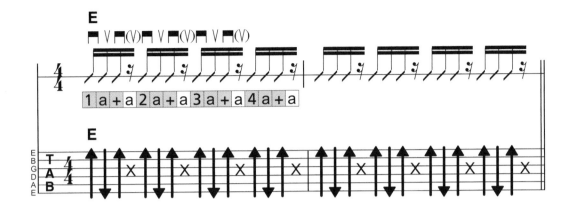

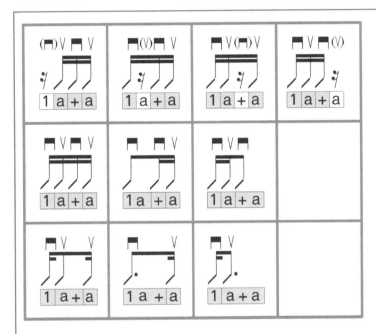

- Speaking the patterns out loud will help you practice. Say: "1 a and a 2 a and a 3 a and a 4 a and a."

- When you see an eighth note, it is important that you count it as exactly two sixteenth notes. (Exception: two or more consecutive eighth notes should still be counted as eighth notes!)

- With sixteenth-note rests, the pattern of alternating up- and down-strokes is broken. In these situations, the "air strumming" technique can be useful (notated above using brackets). This means that instead of actually striking the strings, you imitate the stroke just above the strings. This will help you to stay in tempo.

- The dotted eighth–sixteenth pattern (and it's reverse) can also be spoken out loud:

Daaa–Da–Daaa–Da–Daaa–Da–Daaa–Da. Accent the first, third, fifth syllables.
1   2   3   4

Da–Daaa–Da–Daaa–Da–Daaa–Da–Daaa. Accent the first, third, fifth syllables.
1   2   3   4

Exercises combining different note values

The following exercises will give you a chance to combine the note values you have learned with simple chord changes. Make sure the chord changes are neat and accurate. If you have trouble with the rhythm in bar 1 of the example below, practice it slowly saying "one a and a two a and a three a and a four a and a." Then gradually increase the speed until you get the hang of it.

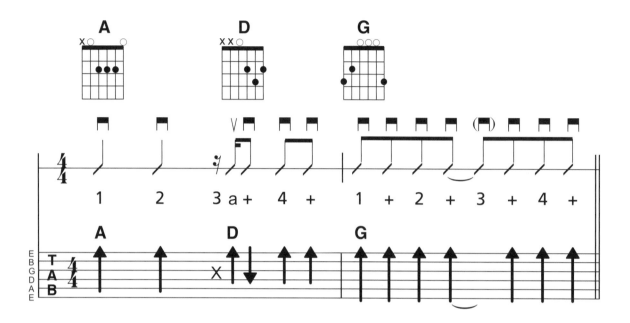

Be careful not to make the sixteenths in the following passage sound too heavy. You will find this easier if you keep your strums light and avoid pulling down too hard on the strings. Practice the rhythm first without your guitar, clapping your hands and tapping your foot on every beat.

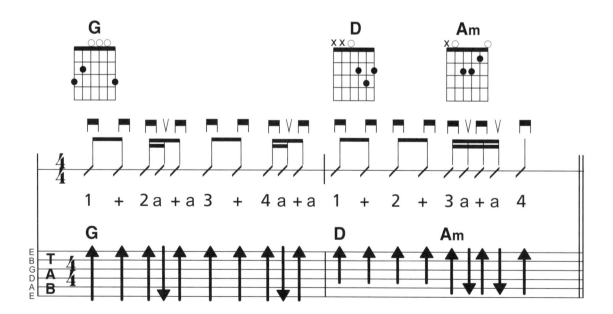

In blues, country, and rock 'n' roll, songs are frequently played using a shuffle rhythm. The term shuffle stems from an African-American dance form. The rhythmic figure is simply the combination of a long and short note. When spoken, it sounds:

Daa Da/Daa Da/Daa Da/Daa Da
1   2   3   4

Due to the potentially untidy way this would be written, the shuffle (or "swing") rhythm is often notated just as straight eighths. This makes the music much easier to read. A symbol signifying that the piece is to be played using a shuffle rhythm is written above the first bar of music. The diagrams below show shuffle eighths and shuffle sixteeths.

As you will notice, the shuffle rhythm is derived from the triplet rhythm (☞ page 23). From this, an eighth-note triplet (☞ page 23) becomes a shuffle rhythm by combining a triplet quarter note (the long note: the sum of two triplet eighths) plus a triplet eighth note (for the short note):

In a similar way, a sixteenth-note triplet becomes an eighth plus a sixteenth:

In the example below, the shuffle rhythm is written as eighth notes grouped in twos. Don't forget, though, that they should sound like triplets!

Notating the shuffle rhythm using eighth notes

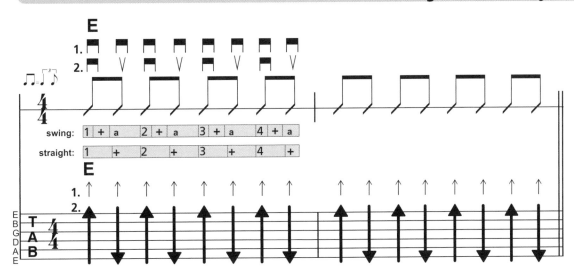

- First, practice the shuffle rhythm using downstrokes

- Next, practice the shuffle rhythm using alternating up- and downstrokes

- Sometimes the shuffle rhythm is represented using the dotted eighth-sixteenth figure: ♪. This figure comes from boogie-woogie, but in practice, reading it as such tends to encourage sixteenth counting. You shouldn't forget that one sixteenth is the equivalent of 25% of a quarter note, whereas each triplet eighth note is worth 33.3% of a quarter note!

Tips

Common time signatures

So far, we have only encountered the time signature ⁴⁄₄ (☞ page 5), but there are many different time signatures, of which the following are the most common in Western music: ²⁄₄, ³⁄₄, ⁶⁄₈, ¹²⁄₈ and ²⁄₂.

The ²⁄₄ bar

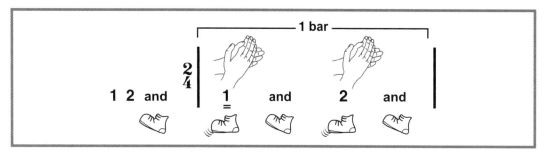

In ²⁄₄ time, "1" is the strong beat and "2" is the weak beat. ²⁄₄ time is particularly common in folk and country music.

The ³⁄₄ bar

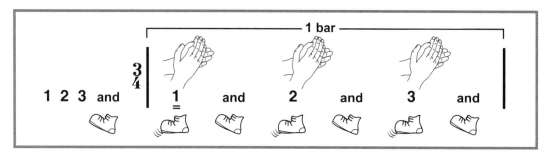

The ³⁄₄ bar is also known as "waltz time." "1" is the strong beat and the "2" and "3" are weak beats.

The ⁶⁄₈ bar

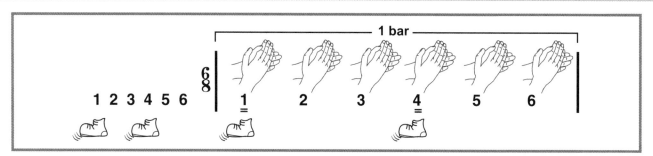

The ⁶⁄₈ bar has two strong beats, "1" and "4." A well-known song in ⁶⁄₈ time is *The House Of The Rising Sun* (☞ *GUITAR SPRINGBOARD: Scales Made Easy*).

The ¹²⁄₈ bar

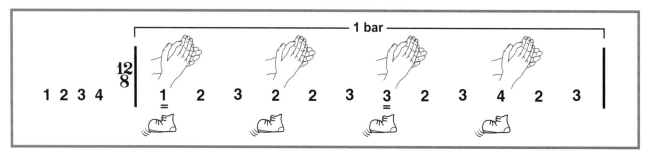

¹²⁄₈, like ⁴⁄₄, has strong beats on "1" and "3." ¹²⁄₈ is commonly used in rock and pop and is useful for notating shuffle rhythms (☞ page 29) as well as being an alternative to writing triplets (☞ page 23).

Summary: basic note and rest values

Notation on a five-line staff	Rhythmic notation	Name and value (1 quarter note = 1 count)	4/4 counting (1 2 3 4)
𝅝		Whole note (duration = 4 quarter notes)	
𝅗𝅥.		Dotted half (duration = 3 quarter notes)	
𝅗𝅥		Half note (duration = 2 quarter notes)	
♩		Quarter note (1 count)	
♪		Eighth note (2 eighths = 1 quarter)	
𝅘𝅥𝅯		Sixteenth note (4 sixteenths = 1 quarter)	
𝅘𝅥𝅰		Thirty-second note (8 thirty-seconds = 1 quarter)	
𝅘𝅥𝅱		Sixty-fourth note (16 sixty-fourths = 1 quarter)	
♩.		Dotted quarter (1 quarter + 1 eighth)	
♪.		Dotted eighth (1 eighth + 1 sixteenth)	
3 ♪♪♪		Eighth-note triplet (duration = 1 quarter)	
3 ♩♩♩		Quarter-note triplet (duration = 2 quarters)	
6	6	Sextuplet (duration = 1 quarter note)	

Notation on a five-line staff and in rhythmic notation	Name and value (1 quarter note = 1 count)	4/4 counting (1 2 3 4)
	Whole rest (4 quarters)	
	Dotted half rest (3 quarters)	
	Half rest (2 quarters)	
𝄽	Quarter rest (1 quarter note)	
𝄾	Eighth rest (1/2 a count)	
𝄿	Sixteenth rest (1/4 of a count)	
𝅀	Thirty-second rest (1/8 of a count)	
𝅁	Sixty-fourth rest (1/16 of a count)	
𝄽.	Dotted quarter rest (1 quarter + 1 eighth)	
𝄾.	Dotted eighth rest (1 eighth + 1 sixteenth)	

Summary: rhythmic notation

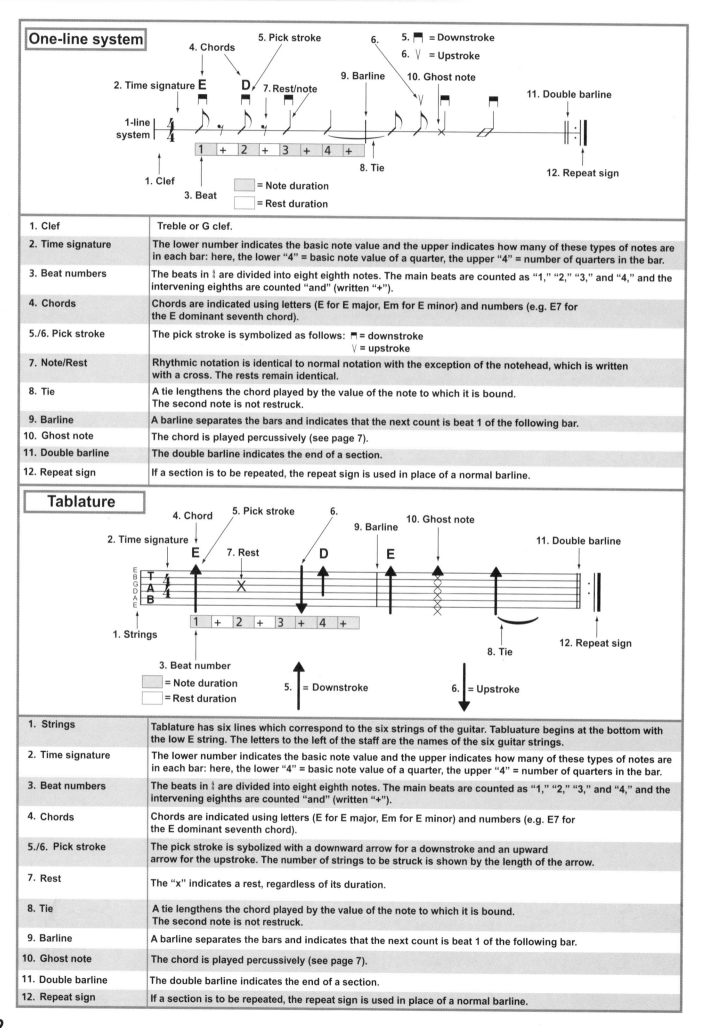

1. Clef	Treble or G clef.
2. Time signature	The lower number indicates the basic note value and the upper indicates how many of these types of notes are in each bar: here, the lower "4" = basic note value of a quarter, the upper "4" = number of quarters in the bar.
3. Beat numbers	The beats in ¼ are divided into eight eighth notes. The main beats are counted as "1," "2," "3," and "4," and the intervening eighths are counted "and" (written "+").
4. Chords	Chords are indicated using letters (E for E major, Em for E minor) and numbers (e.g. E7 for the E dominant seventh chord).
5./6. Pick stroke	The pick stroke is symbolized as follows: ⊓ = downstroke ∨ = upstroke
7. Note/Rest	Rhythmic notation is identical to normal notation with the exception of the notehead, which is written with a cross. The rests remain identical.
8. Tie	A tie lengthens the chord played by the value of the note to which it is bound. The second note is not restruck.
9. Barline	A barline separates the bars and indicates that the next count is beat 1 of the following bar.
10. Ghost note	The chord is played percussively (see page 7).
11. Double barline	The double barline indicates the end of a section.
12. Repeat sign	If a section is to be repeated, the repeat sign is used in place of a normal barline.

1. Strings	Tablature has six lines which correspond to the six strings of the guitar. Tabluature begins at the bottom with the low E string. The letters to the left of the staff are the names of the six guitar strings.
2. Time signature	The lower number indicates the basic note value and the upper indicates how many of these types of notes are in each bar: here, the lower "4" = basic note value of a quarter, the upper "4" = number of quarters in the bar.
3. Beat numbers	The beats in ¼ are divided into eight eighth notes. The main beats are counted as "1," "2," "3," and "4," and the intervening eighths are counted "and" (written "+").
4. Chords	Chords are indicated using letters (E for E major, Em for E minor) and numbers (e.g. E7 for the E dominant seventh chord).
5./6. Pick stroke	The pick stroke is sybolized with a downward arrow for a downstroke and an upward arrow for the upstroke. The number of strings to be struck is shown by the length of the arrow.
7. Rest	The "x" indicates a rest, regardless of its duration.
8. Tie	A tie lengthens the chord played by the value of the note to which it is bound. The second note is not restruck.
9. Barline	A barline separates the bars and indicates that the next count is beat 1 of the following bar.
10. Ghost note	The chord is played percussively (see page 7).
11. Double barline	The double barline indicates the end of a section.
12. Repeat sign	If a section is to be repeated, the repeat sign is used in place of a normal barline.